A Little Book of CHI

Cosmic **H**ealing **I**nspiration

Lifestyle Solutions – Achieving Balance Within

First published in the UK and Ireland in 2008 by

Mercedes Nunns

www.spiritualityinformation.info
Windermere, Cumbria

Conceived, created and designed by
Mercedes Nunns

Copyright © Mercedes Nunns

Text copyright © Mercedes Nunns

Photography for all content - copyright © Mercedes Nunns.
Taken whilst travelling the world.

Design, photography & artwork for the butterfly logo (in colour and black & white) copyright © Mercedes Nunns.

All rights reserved. No part of this publication including photographs may be reproduced or utilised in any other form or by any means electronic or mechanical, including photocopying, recording, or any information storage and retrieval system now known or hereafter invented, without the prior written permission of the publisher and author.

A CIP record for this book is available from the British Library.

ISBN: 978-0-9556907-1-6

£7.99

Printed and bound in Spain.

Introduction

A warm welcome to A Little Book of CHI – a collection of words designed to help you achieve balance within and contribute to your lifestyle solutions.

This little book is designed for anyone and everyone of all ages. Whether you are a young person looking for inspiration, solace, direction in life and hope. You may be an adult who has gone through recent changes and is simply looking for some comforting words that will help you on to a happier path. Perhaps you are a pensioner and wondering how fast the world has changed since you were a young person – perhaps some of these words will give you hope and love about what really matters in life. Whoever you are, the art of healing words contained in this book comes to you with love & a true desire for you to get to a happier place within.

This little book may help you to achieve a more balanced outlook, ascertain where you may have allowed your priorities to go astray and how easily it is to just "think" in a slightly different, simple way to come back to a place of happiness, balance and well-being.

This little book doesn't attempt to present all the answers – it is designed to get you thinking in a peaceful, kind and loving way.

It could be helpful at a time of healing, change, renewed perception, re-evaluation of your life or simply make a lovely gift for someone close to you who may benefit from the words contained in A Little Book of CHI.

Something to keep close by and simply open randomly at any page – allowing that theme to resonate with your mind, body and soul for that moment in time.

With the best intentions to get you on to a happier path – I hope you enjoy this little book.

Mercedes Nunns

A is for - ABUNDANCE

Abundance comes in many forms, it is quite normal to immediately think of abundance in terms of "money". This is quite true but there are many other forms of abundance that are worth noting and realise you can enjoy. Let's start with something that is there for everyone – air – we need that to breath and we need clean air to breath, those who can breath in fresh mountain air or fresh sea air are breathing in the very best for their mind, body and soul. Not everyone can have this pure air, many live in cities and work inside buildings for many hours. Gardens, parks and natural reserves are quite easy to access, so it's beneficial to go for a walk each day, spend time alone in nature and simply allow your natural reserves to be topped up. Water is essential to life and many of us find ourselves drinking bottled mineral water these days as a source of purity and a healthy choice. Bathing in water on a daily basis is a private time of ritual when you prepare your mind, body and soul for the day ahead. An invigorating shower with the right choice of aromatherapy gels is a positive way to start the day. Equally so is a relaxing bath in the evening using Lavender or Camomile to ensure you sleep well and allow your body, mind and soul to regenerate.

The Sun – is the giver of all light and something most people look to – it brings an almost instant happiness to the soul. Many of us cannot live in the sunshine but we try our best to spend at least some of the summer holidays in a sunny place. Spending time in the outdoors gives you an uplifting feeling, so even if it's about doing a little bit of gardening, sitting in the sunshine and sipping a cool glass of water – consider yourself to be living in abundance.

B is for - BENEVOLANCE

Being benevolent comes from a desire to genuinely help others. In doing so this brings about great harmony in your own life and in the life of others. Being benevolent is not always possible though and many people choose not to be benevolent because they feel that they cannot give enough or that their own expectations are too high. Anything, however small and insignificant to you that is given to another person with love and genuine intent is an immeasurable gift.

Being benevolent to oneself is a very good starting point, as you look at yourself in the mirror and realise that there are certain aspects of yourself you still need to give to. This is not selfishness, but a realisation that you need certain energies to come to you. Once you identify this, the universe will present ways you can be benevolent to yourself. As you grow and evolve, you are then in a position to be benevolent to others as you choose and as and when you are able to. If someone asks you for your help and you are not in a position to give it because of time constraints, family and other commitments then saying "no" can be taken as a rejection. Saying "I can't at the moment – sorry, my day/week is full" is a kinder way of saying "no". There are many reasons why help cannot always be given and the person asking for help should not take this personally. It may simply mean when asking for help, you need to do so in a different direction or check the situation again for yourself. Do you really need the help? Is there something you have overlooked? Can you find a solution of your own?

Are you the one giving the help – being benevolent to another is a great responsibility, whether it is simply being a shoulder to cry on, working for or with someone, being a parent or carer. Being a "giver" can be very stressful at times and you may need to identify that you should take some "time out" to regenerate yourself – being mindful of your own needs and allowing time and space to balance your own mind, body and soul.

Benevolence is a two way stretch where sometimes you are the giver and sometimes you are the receiver and sometimes you are both or neither. A flow of energy runs through our lives at different times and karmically we receive and give in many different ways.
Be kind to yourself and be kind to others as you maintain a benevolent balance throughout your life.

C is for - COURAGE

Courage is often seen as being brave in a "bravado" or "male" aspect. Courage is really so much more than this perception. Finding the courage to be silent and learn of our own weaknesses and strengths comes from the ability to know oneself and be able to be strong in a quiet way.

Being able to say what you really feel in a way that is truthful and loving takes great courage. Being able to say "no" in a kind and effective way that explains why you are saying "no" takes great courage. Asking for help takes great courage and saying "I love you" takes great courage.

Courage goes hand in hand with rejection and so many fail to be courageous for fear of being rejected, for fear of choosing the wrong moment or simply not knowing oneself fully.

Being courageous means you can say what you feel and say it because you don't expect anything in return – simply because you feel it. Being courageous also means accepting what another person might want to say to you. Saying "thank you" or showing that you appreciate the courage shown goes a long way to forming a healthy and lasting relationship. It can be with anyone – your parents, siblings, friends, partner or co-workers. This energy will flow back to you in time and you will come to realise that as long as you are courageous in a truthful way, expressing yourself with kindness, then very little can go wrong.

Having courage is about choice and choosing which direction you want to go in and sometimes this can mean leaving the ones you love behind for a while. As you grow and evolve and maintain a happy link with your loved ones – you live in courage. Choosing to return "home" also takes great courage.

D is for - DEPTH

"Depth of feelings", "depth of character", "digging deep". These are all little phrases everyone uses but what do they really mean to you. When we search our own hearts and minds what do we find. Memories of past events, experiences, situations, people we have shared our lives with, places we have lived and places we have visited. How we perceive these events in time and how we allow them to surface from our depths is what shapes the person today. If you choose to read and gain knowledge along the way, it is possible to become a much deeper person, however sharing that knowledge and allowing others in to that depth gives meaning to that knowledge.

Everyone has something deep inside that we choose not to reveal to the world – perhaps because we fear rejection or that simply we are surprised to find – everyone else does agree and the idea or thought really wasn't that deep after all. When we share our inner most thoughts and feelings with close friends and family, it has a direct influence on those people. We must carefully choose which thoughts and feelings we share openly to ensure our influence is a positive one.

Many times in our lives we doubt ourselves, our abilities and wonder what it is we are here to do or be. Being positive about our deepest desires, feelings and thoughts means that there is greater chance of them manifesting in to reality and being enjoyed in the true light of day.

Whatever your deepest feelings, thoughts and desires are, first write them down – be definitive and then allow the universe to bring the next steps to you.

E is for - EVOLUTION

Evolution is a process we all experience in small ways throughout our lives. Learning to cope with changes – some of our own choosing and others a consequence of situations that we have no control over. As we learn to evolve, we learn to accept. Accepting our situation, ourselves as we are today is something that requires a way of looking at things positively. Taking experiences in to account we also learn that setting our boundaries of what we will and will not accept, allows us to evolve too.

As our life evolves around cycles, we come to recognise similarities as the energy around us ebbs and flows in and out. We realise that sharing is a large part of our evolution and that our human connections become ever more important to us. Family, friends – old and new as well as our co-workers are all links to our personal and collective evolution. What we learn from each other and what we teach each other has great effect. Travelling the world allows us to see things much more clearly and the realisation that family and close friends are what forms most communities. Evolution allows new ideas and ways of looking at ourselves, others and the world around us. Positive thoughts and ideas are always good for our evolution. Setting a ripple of positive effect through words of love, praise and positivity brings a greater sense of purpose and meaning to all our lives.

As we evolve we learn to achieve balance within our own minds, hearts and souls, bringing a sense of happiness.

F is for - FAITH

Faith in God, faith in the Universe, faith in oneself, faith in your family, faith in your friends. Faith is something that cannot easily be explained. We choose to "believe" in many things throughout our lives. Perhaps we are born in to a culture where the belief system is already chosen for you, growing up with a set of principles that help you and guide you through life.

As we grow, leave the safety and love of our family, or choose to leave because of work, wanting our personal freedom or simply to find another way we feel is better for us, we take some of that faith with us. Faith is simply what we choose to believe in. Believing that you are strong and able and can achieve the things you want in life is faith; believing that God will take care of you and guide you along your path is faith; believing that the oracles you consult and choose for guidance will point you in the right direction is faith; listening to the little voice inside your mind is faith. Following your heart is faith.

Sometimes we need to share our thoughts and through faith we find the guidance we seek. Faith gives us strength that at times is immeasurable and we receive help from the most amazing people or situations. Having faith that you will always be alright and that the "universe" is on your side means you have every chance of making your dreams come true.

G is for - GRATITUDE

Showing gratitude and receiving gratitude is a gift within a gift. The gift of giving and receiving requires an ability to give without expecting anything in return and to receive graciously.

These are qualities that are not easy to show or be. When we give something it makes us feel good about ourselves, we are giving something to someone that we know has been deserving of that gift, we may even know that the gift we are giving that person is something they truly want and need and therefore it makes the action even more meaningful. Receiving that gift can bring joy and utter amazement to the receiver, especially if they weren't expecting it. Being able to receive and say thank you and let your heart, smile and eyes show that gratitude is another gift that reflect back to the giver.

Balancing these attributes out within oneself is the key to knowing how to give and receive and feel good about both aspects. Part of letting go of a situation or person is simply giving their freedom and taking your freedom in return. Allowing you and the other person the time and space required.

Being grateful for the simple things in life like the sunshine, air, water, beauty, family and friends are a way of giving a gift to yourself every day and in many moments of that day.

Taking these amazing gifts for granted is something that we have all been guilty of at times in our lives and often the universe reminds us in gentle ways and sometimes not.

Being grateful, knowing how to give and receive with grace and love is a gift everyone has, does and is.

H is for - HOPE

"Hope springs eternal" – is a well used phrase throughout time. It is often seen as pointless to be hopeful, however when we choose to have hope, we allow ourselves to work towards that which we have hope in. It can be anything – to have our loving soul mate find us, to have a child, to find a new home, to get the job we always dreamed of, to be happy and content with all that we are and have in life. Hope is something that is there for everyone.

Hope gives us the strength to strive for what we wish for, that which we feel will make us happy or make our lives more comfortable or enjoyable. Hoping helps us to set our standards, make things better and work for something we know we can attain.

Being hopeful for others is a great gift too. It means we are hopeful that our closest friends and family will always be alright, will always be safe, live happily and be able to cope with every day things. Hoping for the best for another person means allowing that other person to be able to make their own choices and that those choices are right for them. Our choices – the ones we make for ourselves should also be blessed by our closest family and friends with a wish of hope.

Being hopeful for ourselves and others brings a positive energy all round and makes anything possible.

I is for - INTUITION

Intuition is something everyone has. It is our guiding power that comes from deep within our hearts and deep within our minds. Connecting our heart and minds and finding quiet moments to ask about our life questions.

Many people choose not to tap in to their own intuition for fear of what their answers might be. As we grow and learn about the depths of our minds we may find ourselves going in to places we never knew existed and this can cause fear. However if through love we choose to venture and explore the vast entity of our minds, we find the most beautiful places, most beautiful solutions and most peaceful and harmonious light.

Looking to those who have a great awareness of their own intuition is very helpful to those who are still searching for their own. Looking to a teacher, counsellor or anyone who has found the light within, will always be willing to assist you.

Be willing to dive in to your own heart and mind, even after consultation with your chosen "guide". Combining the information you have received from your guide and the information your heart and mind brings, helps you to tune in and make the right decisions for yourself.

Everyone, from time to time in life, chooses a "guide" – it can be a trusted member of your family or a close friend, a spiritual person or someone who is well respected by the community. Sometimes a total stranger can say something to us and it resonates so loudly that we can only think this person was sent by some divine force to help us.

Intuition is a sacred and beautiful gift within each and every one of us.

J is for - JOY

Joy is a feeling around our hearts that makes us smile, our eyes light up and our spirits lift. Anything and anyone can cause it – it might be something very simple like your pet cat or dog with its beautiful bright eyes waiting for you or looking up at you and reminding you how much love they have for you. It might be your partner who has waited patiently for you to return home so they can eat a meal with you and chat about your respective day. Joy comes in many forms – small, medium, large, expected and unexpected. It's the unexpected moments that can often bring the most joy but let us stop and think a moment about the expected moments, the ones we anticipate every day and look forward to – the small ones. Taking that first sip of tea or coffee in the morning, drinking a glass of water after a sporting session, seeing a friend for lunch, taking your dog for a walk. Beautiful moments that happen every day in your life – these are what Joy is.

Joy is found in laughter – people, situations, memories that make you laugh, bring moments of Joy. Waking up in the morning and saying "it's going to be a good day today" brings a sense of Joy.

Joy is found in our friendships as we share precious thoughts, feelings and time together. Family bring joy – our father who makes us laugh, the brother who is naturally witty, the sister who mixes up her words and has everyone falling around in laughter, the mother who cooks wonderful meals and has everyone seated together. The youngest member of the family – the grand-child who has learnt new ways of finding making people laugh brings a flow of love and joy and the baby who gurgles, smiles and senses a loving environment grows in Joy.

K is for - KARMA

Karma is something that some people believe in, some people don't believe and some don't have any opinion about. We are learning every day what Karma really means. Believing that if we do good things we will receive good karma, or by doing bad things we will receive bad things is a very simplistic way of looking at karma. If someone hurts you and you cry – this is karmic within itself, for that person has brought pain to your heart and in turn must realise that this reflects back to them. When someone makes you laugh, it is infectious and they will probably laugh as well.

Karma is a reflection of our hearts, minds and souls. Being kind and helpful to those we care about and strangers who pass us by, gives our hearts a sense of well being. Being taken advantage of – makes us feel used. Balancing our karma and allowing our boundaries to be set is a good way of dealing with the natural way of karma.

Giving and receiving forms part of the karmic balance, our thoughts and feelings have a great karmic effect. How we react to events, people and situations all have a karmic effect. If someone has the better of you and you decide to let them go from your life – you effectively break that karma and move on. Along the path of life you may receive credits for good deeds done or you may leave yourself open to inviting a person in to your life who is worthy of your love, attention and friendship.

Karma works in many different ways and it is "how" we choose to look at life that brings about positive or negative karma. Every event, however large or small involves a flow of karma. Seeing the positive side of life, your life and those around you helps to bring a positive karmic effect.

L is for - LOVE

Love is the ultimate power. The force that binds us and brings happiness, joy, laughter, positivity and hope. Our ability to have faith in love is what always wins through. Love comes from the heart but also from the mind – the ability to see things in a compassionate light – feeling a situation and seeing a person in their true light.

Love is love and there are many degrees. The love we have within our families is bound by circumstance, unbreakable bonds and ancestors. If these are carefully nurtured, we find friendship, understanding, learning, teaching, sharing and a caring environment in which we can grow and live.

Love outside our family sometimes takes much longer. The romantic sense of falling in love can happen in a heart beat, but the love and friendship that grows over time has a deeper sense and often lasts a lifetime. The love and deep affection we have for our friends involves experiences shared, conversations, problems, experiences, giving and receiving and a faith that our friendship is bound by a respect and understanding that is enveloped by love.

Love yourself – something people often find hard to achieve. When we learn to love ourselves, give ourselves the correct nurturing, time, space and nutrition we are achieving a love of self. When we are happy and comfortable with this, we can easily love another and form a balanced and happy partnership. Loving someone else comes second to loving oneself –this way we are totally in the light of love.

M is for - MERCY

Mercy is compassion. Mercy is something that is given at moments that are most felt by two people. Showing or giving mercy means one person must be able to see and feel the heart of another or others. We are all capable of being merciful but putting this in to action can so often involve some sort of self-sacrifice.

Mercy can be shown in small ways, simply making someone a cup of tea because you know they are tired, have had a long day and will find it a refreshing and gratifying gift. Mercy is being considerate of another person. Being merciful – showing compassion is something that many people simply refuse to do or be mainly because they are so hurt or caught up in their own agenda. Yet a selfless act of mercy can bring healing to the person showing mercy as well as to the one receiving.

When we find ourselves on the receiving end of someone who is showing mercy, we can only feel that we are being taken care of and that a higher force is ensuring we are protected. Giving thanks and showing gratitude for this moment brings positivity to your life and those around you.

N is for - NATURE

Nature is real – it is there for everyone to see, feel and enjoy. Our natural surroundings are what bring a sense of joy, hope, faith and love to our hearts. Being out in nature is good for the soul. Walking and breathing in the fresh air can make all the difference between having a good day and having a bad day. Starting your day with a walk – even if that walk is to take you to work, means you become one with nature for a while and replenish your natural energies.

Trees, fields, meadows, forests, glades, ponds, lakes and gardens entwine throughout our countryside and world. The seas meet the shores and form sandy beaches where we can spend many happy times. The pathways through our woodlands and forests are places of inspiration as we experience the cool shade of those protective trees and marvel at the golden rays of sunshine that stream through the branches. The leaves on the trees are magical as they twinkle, rustle and gently sway in the breeze. Noticing the birds singing and chirping as they perch themselves up high, swoop and circle and balance on the waves of the wind shows us that the universe is truly supportive of all living beings.

Being in nature puts us in touch with our higher self, brings a sense of well being and helps to bring clarity of thought.

Meditating in the open brings innovation, solutions and peace.

O is for - OPENESS

Being open simply means allowing yourself to be aware and notice what is going on around you. People, places, situations all require that we are aware so that we may learn and grow further.

A willingness to be open requires courage and the ability to show our feelings and share our thoughts. In this way we are better able to benefit through positivity.

We can choose to see things in a positive light and being more open with our hearts and minds, then means we can share our positivity with others. The ripple effect of this is immeasurable and only brings joy and harmony.

As we stretch our arms out and invite others to us, we find new friendships forming, new energy and a new emphasis on life. As we remain open we find that our family and established friends are better able to benefit from our positive outlook and in return be uplifted.

Keeping ourselves open is no easy task as life throws many things at us, we feel threatened or we are tired or overloaded by our daily life. Taking a walk in nature, finding a way to have a 5 minute meditation or attend a yoga class are all ways of helping you to be open, positive and happy. Lots of people love to do sports and this is another way of keeping a balance and being more open.

P is for PATIENCE

"Patience is a virtue – seldom in a woman, never in a man". This famous phrase is used endless times by many people. Increasingly though we find ourselves in the presence of men and women who have not learnt to be patient.

Patience can only come with time, experience or an innate wisdom that if you are lucky – you are born with and keep. Being patient is showing you are willing to wait for something or someone, for events to unfold at their own pace and for the flow of energy to simply form around you and bring you exactly the right things.

The Universe loves to serve patience, but so many times it will bring something to people that they find surprising, joyful and amazing.

Our lesson is to learn patience through understanding our own thoughts, desires and feelings. As we grow and gain years, noting our experiences along the way, we start to have a chance at being patient.

When we nurture patience and allow it to be in our lives, the most amazing situations unfold, the most worthwhile friendships form and longer lasting love is possible.

Showing you are sensitive to others feelings, respecting their thoughts and allowing the right time and space to flow between you brings a patient nature.

Q is for - QUANTUM LEAP

We often hear of the phrase "Quantum Leap of Faith". This is something that requires a great deal of courage and strength. Quantum Physics is often perceived as being the truth and the key to how the Universe works.

Sometimes we feel that we totally know something – we cannot say why or how but we just know something. If that feeling is so strong and we act upon it and stay strong, we find a whole new dimension in living. We may have to accept that our family and friends don't necessarily agree or understand our thoughts, feelings and actions BUT if what we decide to do is in the light of love and we don't give up – it can only bring love and joy. If we ask our closest family and friends to have a little patience and allow our vision to unfold we ask for a positive flow of energy which propels our visions, hopes and desires forward.

Taking that Quantum Leap means taking that first step, knowing that it is a first step to our vision, dream and a better way of living. It doesn't mean we have to take a leap in to the darkness of the unknown. There are many ways we can take a Quantum Leap and still maintain a balance, stability and daily routine that allows us to feel secure whilst pursuing our dreams. Balancing our daily commitments and slowly growing our vision, simply means putting a little time aside each day to nurture and feed our vision. A Quantum Leap simply requires us to have a vision, nurture it and allow it to evolve and grow. Success comes after time.

R is for - RESPECT

Respect starts with "self". The only way to grow a respectful life, community and inner circle is to start with oneself. Respecting ourselves through our demeanour, actions, principles and behaviour are all good starting points on the road of respect.

As we grow and learn to respect ourselves, we allow for our own limitations, our own endless possibilities and our own thoughts and feelings to have time to grow. Respect is allowing ourselves to have a balanced approach to every day life. Work, play, time for nourishing our bodies and quality time with our family and friends and time alone, all form our ability to respect ourselves.

Our personal set of principles will decide on the level of respect we receive from others. This can become quite complicated depending on the belief system we have been born in to and live within. In some belief systems the oldest member of the male in the family has automatic respect; in others it is the mother figure. In many it is the formation of the family that brings respect as we learn and evolve through guidance from our parents. Teachers are respected for their knowledge and ability to teach children as they grow up. Our chosen guides and masters through life are given respect – for their humility, knowledge and kindness.

All these examples are something that we can take for ourselves and ultimately grow the seeds of respect within ourselves, family, friends, working connections and the community. This ripple effect brings a new realm of harmony in the world. Each one of us is responsible for respecting ourselves and giving respect to others.

S is for - SHARING

Sharing involves two or more people. The fun part about sharing is someone gets to give something and the other gets to receive. Now the obvious result of this is that the person who receives, then feels that they want to give but often the one who gives, doesn't necessarily want to receive or may find it more difficult to receive. A natural giver must learn that the art of sharing, requires that they receive gifts too. Sharing requires two flows of energy and should be done with love and good intentions.

There are many ways to share with your family and friends, it can so often simply mean spending time together, communicating thoughts and feelings through conversation, laughter and sharing experiences. A time of sharing can be sitting and having a meal together as a family, enjoying food and talking about the day. Couples need to find time to share in this busy world and children need to share time with their parents to evolve and feel the love and support.

Friends share time together, enjoying each other's company, being influenced by each other's experiences, thoughts and feelings.

Sometimes we might choose to share something with a total stranger. We find ourselves sitting on a train or plane and offer a sweet to the person sitting next to us, they may in return ask us if we would like to read the paper they have finished with. Sharing can be very simple and help to make your daily routine a little more enjoyable. Sometimes we get to make a new friend by sharing.

Sharing comes from the heart and is an ability to be able to give and receive with grace and love.

T is for - TRUST

Trust takes time. Sometimes we can instantly know that we can trust someone – but this is rare. Trust takes years of learning and knowing. Our family members are part of our lives from the moment we are born – these are the people we come to trust first. As we grow and learn, we put our trust in our teachers and once we step out in to the working world, we put our trust in our mentors and people of authority. We learn to trust those who hold a position of responsibility and hope that they will guide us correctly.

Sometimes we simply have to look inside ourselves to know if we can trust another person or situation. If we are in the flow of love and light and all intentions are good, we take a step forward and trust. Loyalty to our friends and to ourselves involves a decree of trust. As time passes this bond of trust grows and can become a source of strength.

Trust involves each person really knowing themselves, understanding and accepting our hopes, desires, limitations and possibilities. When we place time and knowledge together we come to trust.

When we share with our family and friends we grow the bonds of trust and loyalty.

U is for - UNDERSTANDING

Understanding requires that we know ourselves and accept our family and friends as they are. We come to an understanding as we grow and learn from one another, bringing about a positive evolution of our circle of connections, community and the world at large.

Part of being able to show understanding involves having an empathic approach to other people. Knowing what it feels like to be sad, to lose someone or something we really cherished, to get that new job, to move to a new home, to feel euphoric. As we experience these feelings ourselves through life, we are better able to understand others in our lives and show understanding.

When we read or learn something new, we may instantly feel that we understand and that the words resonate with us. As we grow and learn, we come to unlock the secrets of the universe and accept that the energy flows in our favour, most of the time. Accepting this brings a greater awareness of understanding.

Showing empathy and understanding to others in a kind and humble way, brings enlightenment, joy and love to you and those you are connected to.

V is for - VICTORY

Victory means – knowing we already have everything that we require for a happy, harmonious and joyful life. Knowing we are loved and able to give love and appreciate all the people in our lives.

Gaining victory over something means you don't allow a situation or experience get the better of you. Seeing every experience, situation and connection as a flow of energy and taking the positivity out of it, brings victory.

As we learn and grow through our lives, we learn to live in victory. The more we know ourselves and connect with love and joy to those around us, we live in victory.

Victory is not about winning – sometimes knowing when to walk away, brings internal victory and freedom. Keeping connections with those who love us, allow us to love and bring trust, loyalty, friendship, sharing and respect to all those connections means victory.

W is for - WISDOM

Wisdom usually comes with time, experience and age. We are all born with an innate wisdom but don't always tap in to this wisdom until we have experienced life, relationships, experiences, situations and quite simply lived a little or a lot ☺.

Wisdom brings peace and contentment. A harmony that lives in our hearts and gives joy and peace on a daily basis. Not wanting too much and learning that less is more, brings wisdom.

Knowing we can achieve certain things in our life and that certain things will come with time, patience and learning gives us wisdom.

We can share words of wisdom, feelings and thoughts with our loved ones, but ultimately wisdom is a place we find in our hearts that makes us content, at peace with ourselves, our connections and the world around us. Wisdom is something we cannot touch – it's almost beyond an emotion or even a thought – wisdom is a higher level of just "knowing" and "being".

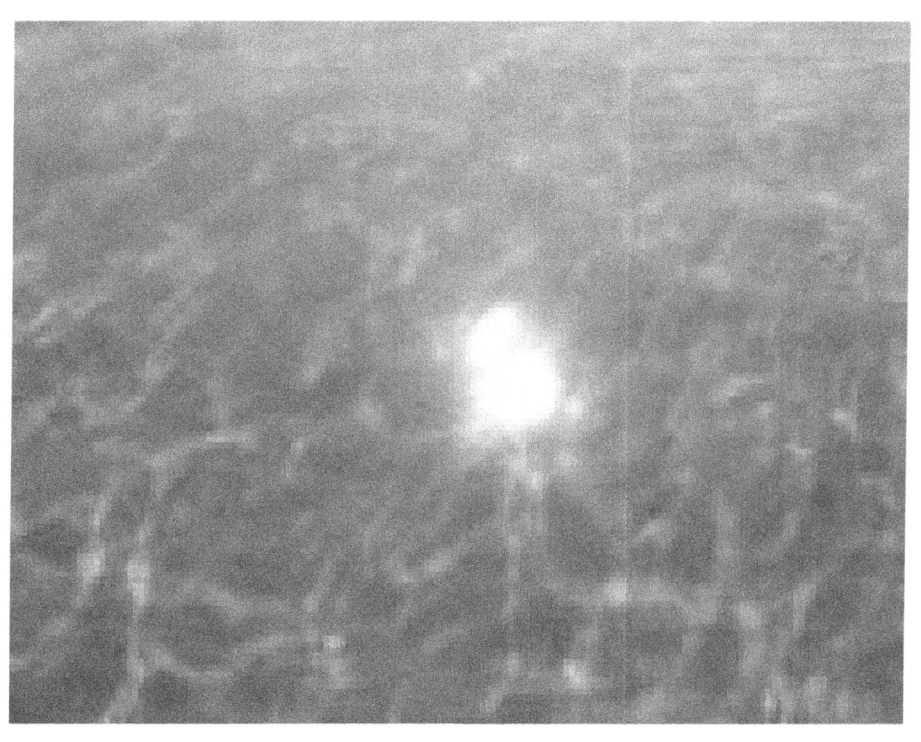

X is for - XENIA

Xenia is a Greek word which means "hospitality". It takes in to account the meaning of a guest or stranger, who is visiting your home, community or country.

There are times in our lives when we find ourselves meeting strangers or have the opportunity to entertain guests and friends. Showing that we are hospitable to the guests that come to our home is a part of being welcoming and showing love and respect.

Being hospitable is a wonderful way of sharing your home, time and sitting with your guests. Learning from each other and perhaps sharing a meal together.

Incorporating many of the main positive attributes of ourselves through sharing, showing respect, learning from one another, eating together, laughing together - we then become more hospitable and open our homes and hearts to others.

Y is for - YIN YANG

Yin Yang is the Chinese word for Balance. We quite simply learn to achieve balance within as we become more experienced at dealing with the ebb and flow of energy that exists within us and in the world around us.

Keeping a balance requires us to share our time in the best way possible to bring harmony, joy and peace in to our lives.

Work and pleasure have an ever increasing pull on our time – we require both to exist and live happily. Sometimes a degree of self-sacrifice is required so that we can achieve something we wish for in life. Redressing the balance as soon as we are able brings healing for the times we could not give to ourselves. Time, rest, nourishment and space are required on a daily basis to bring balance to our lives.

The male and female forces that exist within each of us, form our Yin Yang or balance. Our relationships with our partners, help to form our Yin Yang and learning to flow within our relationships help to bring balance to our lives.

Ensuring our mind, body and soul is in balance is our responsibility, bringing harmony to our lives, relationships and experiences.

Z is for - ZEN

Being ZEN means we have come to a point in our lives where we accept the flow of energy that exists in ourselves and in others around us. When we are Zen we are in harmony, we have achieved balance, we experience love and joy on a daily basis and simply move through time at exactly the right pace. Being happy with who we are, knowing we have all that we require and trusting that the universe is our gift.

Realising the synchronicity of how the universe works, brings about people who are ZEN. It is the secret and the key to having Quantum faith and receiving your heart's desires.

Being Zen is achievable and real.

A Quick Recap

A is for ABUNDANCE

B is for BENEVOLANCE

C is for COURAGE

D is for DEPTH

E is for EVOLUTION

F is for FAITH

G is for GRATITUDE

H is for HOPE

I is for INTUITION

J is for JOY

K is for KARMA

L is for LOVE

M is for MERCY

N is for NATURE

O is for OPENESS

P is for PATIENCE

Q is for QUANTUM LEAP

R is for RESPECT

S is for SHARING

T is for TRUST

U is for UNDERSTANDING

V is for VICTORY

W is for WISDOM

X is for XENIA

Y is for YIN YANG

Z is for ZEN

If you enjoyed this book and it helped to bring inspiration, encouragement, some positive lifestyle solutions and a sense of balance within, then you may also enjoy the following title by Mercedes Nunns

"33 Ways to Keep Your Man Happy – *lucky in love*"

Mercedes Maria Nunns – Spiritual Writer

Acknowledgements

The author wishes to thank her supportive, loving family, wonderful partner, friends and neighbours. Expressing her extreme gratitude to everyone.

Putting together "A Little Book of CHI" took many years of travel, experiences, writing, exploring and researching. It helped me to self-heal & hopefully it will be enjoyed by many & spread happiness and harmony.

Namaste.

Mercedes ☺

www.ingramcontent.com/pod-product-compliance
Lightning Source LLC
Chambersburg PA
CBHW061247040426
42444CB00010B/2278